A Misunderstood Reformer

Sayyid Ahmad Shaheed

Abul Hasan Ali Nadwi

Nadwi Press

2022 CE – 1443 H

Translation of the Qur'ān

It should be perfectly clear that the Qur'ān is only authentic in its original language, Arabic. Since perfect translation of the Qur'ān is impossible, we have used the translation of the meaning of the Qur'ān throughout the book, as the result is only a crude meaning of the Arabic text.

Qur'ānic verses appear in speech marks proceeded by a reference to the Surah and verse number. Sayings (*Hadith*) of Prophet Muhammad (saw) appear in inverted commas along with reference to the Hadith Book and its Reporter.

INDEX

INTRODUCTION

The martyrs, reformers and preachers of Islam were those pure-hearted souls who had dedicated every whit of their lives to God and glorification of His Word. For these men had nothing to do with the world and what it contains, they were able to lay down their lives without the least concern for any fear or favour. They had so eschewed every worldly temptation that they had dismissed from their thoughts the praises to be lavised on them by the future generations, acknowledgement of their services by the coming historians and writers, the eulogies to be sung in their honour by the poets and minstrels and the memorials to be raised by the kings and rulers to pay tribute to them. They dwell in peace with their Lord and are satisfied with the recompense that God alone can bestow on them. Has not the Lord himself said :

"And their Lord hath heard them (and He saith) : Lo : I suffer not the work of any worker, male or female, to be lost. You proceed one from another. So those who fled and were driven forth from their homes and suffered damage for My cause, and fought and were slain, verily I shall remit their evil deeds from them and verily I shall bring them into Gardens underneath which rivers flow. A reward from Allah.   And with Allah is the fairest of rewards.[1]"

Had these devoted and truthful slaves of God been given the choice to make their selection between the blushing honours and nameless obscurity, they would have certainly opted for the latter and entreated God with tears in their eyes to keep their efforts hidden from their fellow beings for being recompensed by Him. There had been men among them who felt disappointed if any of their noble acts came to be known by others. If they ever made a mention of their services unconsciously or under a sudden impulse, they always felt so sorry for it as if they had given out some closely guarded secret.   Bukhārī relates on the authority of Abū Huraira that Abū Mūsā al-Ash'ari once told him : "We accompanied the Prophet on an expedition when we were six in number but had only one camel with us.   We rode it by turns with the result that our feet got injured.   My own feet got hurt with scratches and cuts and the nails of my feet came apart ; we bandaged our wounds with rags and hence the expedition came to be known as *Dhāt-ar-Riq'a*[2]".   Abū Huraira further says that Abū Musā al-Ash'ari narrated the incident but he seemed to feel qualmish, for he hastily added, " I should not have told it."   This shows that Abū Mūsā al-Ash'ari did not want the people to know of the hardship undergone by him in the way of God.

1.   Q. III : 195
2.   *Sahih Bukhārī, Kitāb ul-Maghāzi,* Chap.   *Dhāt-ar-Riq'a,*

(3)

There would be no harm at all, from the point of view of these precursors of faith, if the subsequent generations remained uninformed of their services and sacrifices, since, they felt satisfied that the Lord for whom they had plunged into difficulties wes well-informed of what they had done.

There is another incident relating to the capture of Nahavand[1] which throws light on the way they looked at things.

Historians relate that fierce battle raged during the first few days at Nahavand but at last God granted victory to the Muslims. The commander of the Muslim army sent someone to communicate the good news of victory to the Caliph, 'Umar b. al-Khattāb, and also to inform him that the Commander-in-Chief, N'umān b. Muqran, had been killed in the battle. When the messenger told 'Umar al-Khattāb about the martyrdom of N'umān, he dissolved into tears and asked about others who had been slain in the battle. The messenger told a few names and then said, ''Amīr-ul-Mūminīn, there are many more whom you do not know.'' 'Umar replied weepingly, ''What have they to lose if 'Umar does not know them. God certainly knows all of them[2].''

But, it behoves a man of upright nature that he should acknowledge the favours done to him by a well-wisher. And, if such a benefactor had rendered some service to one's people or nation or died a martyr's death

---

1. A city of Iran where the battle was fought in 641-42 A. H.
2. Ibn Jarir Tabri, *Tārīkh Tabri*, Vol. IV, p. 235.

for the defence of a faith or an ideology or a country, then the memory of such a ministering angel deserves to be commemorated. All the nations of the world possessing a sense of propriety try to keep alive the memory of their benefactors according to their customs and usages. This is the well-known way to pay the debt of gratitude owed to such heroes and to acknowledge their services. The younger generation is enabled, in this manner, to know the great deeds of its forefathers and to derive inspiration from them. The custom of erecting memorials in of honour the 'Unknown Soldiers' prevalent among the nations of the West, signifies nothing but the expression of this gratefulness.

The followers of the prophets and especially the Muslims have an inclination greater than others to show gratitude to their benefactors. Even God has cited, in the Qur'ān, the gratitude shown by the faithful to their predecessors.

"And those who came (into the faith) after them say : Our Lord ! Forgive us and our brethren who were before us in the faith, and place not in our hearts any rancour toward those who believe. Our Lord ! Thou art Full of Pity, Merciful.[1]"

As against this, the people who enter the Hell accuse and call evil upon their precursors since they are an ungrateful lot.

"Every time a nation entereth, in curseth its sister (nation) till, when they have all been made to

---

1. Q. LIX : 10.

(5)

follow one another thither.[1]"

Still, with all this interest and inclination and admiration for the men of great achievements and noble qualities, there are several of them who have yet to be restored their rightful place in the gallary of our heroes. The services and achievements of these men have either not been brought to light or injustice has been done by showing stinted thankfulness to them.

In some cases even fictions of monstrous lies have been woven round their characters in order to conceal their true character and deeds from the gaze of the world.

Shallow and superficial studies, styled as researches, have been another cause for the improper evaluation of the character and achievement of these noblest specimen of humanity. These half-backed studies and half-learned tracts have, without doubt, been more harmful than blind and nacked ignorance for the simple reason that a smattering of knowledge not unoften decieves and misguides whereas unacquaintedness very often prods one to go ahead and lift the veil of secret.

The great renovator of Islam and fighter for its cause that Saiyid Ahmad Shahīd was, ranks among those select and heavenly souls who were supremely blessed with an unshakable faith in God and His promises and had an implicit belief in the life after death. God had also cleansed his heart from the defilements of falseness, vanity and vain pretensions. The world and all its wealth, power

1. Q. VII : 38.

and pelf, were to him valueless like dust. When the Saiyid was staying at Calcutta before embarking the ship for the *haj*, Gulām Husain Khān made bold to say, "The ship you are going in is an ordinary one. It would be proper if you go by the ship "Atīur-Rahmān' which has sixty cannons on board and is captained by Muhammad Husain Turk who holds the charge of forty ships. If you go to Arabia by it, the people there would think more highly of you."

This suggestion made the Saiyid's blood boil in anger. He said in reply, "What did you say, Ghulām Husain Khān ! Honour is given by God and not by man. I regard the esteem and reverence of this world as a dead dog!"

The Saiyid so detested worldly fame and honour that had earnestly prayed God that no trace of his grave might remain after his death. And, so it happened for God did not allow his sepulchre to be known and made a place of adoration by the coming generations.

Viewed in this context, the Saiyid does not require that his successors, scholars, penmen and historians should either study and evaluate the efforts he had made for the revival of Islam or trace the effects of his Movement on the later revivalist and reformatory movements. But the present generation of this *Millat*, and those to come later on, do need to make a close study of his accomplishments impartially and justly, so as to allocate him the place he deserves in the history of Islam. This is an obligation we owe to him, and the sooner we discharge it, the better it would be for us.

These were my thoughts and feelings which urged me to present the life of this great son of Islam before others—to acquit myself of the duty lying on me. Fortunately, I have also had the advantage of having access to certain original sources, not available to others, and also the opportunity to study the Saiyid's life and mission at close quarters. I had, therefore, been giving thought to the matter from a comparatively early age and also written a monograph on the subject. Later on, my studies in connection with the lives of great refomers and renovators of Islam, which have since taken the shape of the *Saviours of Islamic Spirit*, helped me to understand the real worth and value of the Saiyid's Movement and the place he occupies among the luminnaries of Islam. All these considerations prompted me to present this brief account of the Saiyid's life and achievements. May be that someone is moved to take up a more detailed and thorough study of the subject which would undoubtedly be found inspiring by those who are engaged in fighting the battle of Islam against the new ignorance of this Age.

An opportunity for writing this paper was afforded to me when, in 1976, Mohiuddin Ahmad, asked me to write an introduction for his valuable work, *Saiyid Ahmed Shahīd—His Life* and *Mission*. The task being most welcome to me I wrote a rather lengthy introduction in which I drew attention to and protested against the biased and extremely intolerant attitude of the Western writers in regard to the Saiyid and his mission. I tried to show that dearth of material was not the cause of their partisan and unwarranted observations, as it so often happens in depicting the true character and achievements of tne reformers of old. For in such cases, these writers usually exercise their whimsical speculation to present a character-sketch. The introduction was included in the book and also published in some of the Urdu Journals.

I, later on, happened to go through a few Arabic works and journals, reviewing either the Saiyid's Movement or referring to him in some other context. I was amazed to see that instead of taking pains to study the subject all these writers and relied on Western writers. It was so painful to me that I could not take up any other literary work until I had enlarged the aforementioned introduction into its present form. The article written in Arabic suitably incorporated the introduction in English with some additions and alterations. This paper in Arabic was brought out in 1978 by the Nadwatul 'Ulamā, Press under the caption. ''The Great Leader who has been denied justice and due appreciation.'' Its second edition was published by Dār-ul-A 'itasām of Cairo and was warmly received all over the Arab world.

As I felt that this paper succinctly brought out the salient features of the Saiyid' s character and call which would be found useful by those who do not have time to go through more detailed works, I desired my nephew, late Saiyid Mohammad al-Hasanī, the ex-editor of *Al-B'ath al-Islāmī* to render it into Urdu. His translation in Urdu was, as usual, fluent and forceful. Some more additions were however, made by me while going through the Urdu version, which, translated into English

(9)

by Mohiuddin Ahmad, is now in the hands of the readers. I hope that it would be read with interest, and fulfil the purpose for which it has been written.

<table>
<tr><td>Dāira Shāh 'Alam Ullah,
   Rae Bareli.
   September 15, 1979.</td><td>S. Abul Hasan 'Ali.</td></tr>
</table>

A Misunderstood Reformer

The Extensive Field of Reform and Renovation

In its comprehensiveness and mass appeal, and the methodology closely following the prophetic pattern, no contemporary revivalist movement comparable to the powerful movement of Islamic revival headed by Saiyid Ahmad Shahīd, is to be found in the nineteenth century. Even in the preceding few centuries one fails to find any disciplined body of such a sincere, dedicated and godly-minded persons. So widespread and far-reaching were the efforts of Saiyid's followers—practising and preaching the true faith to the masses, guiding and training them through their precepts and sermons and enkindling the spirit of sacrifice in the populace by setting a noble example of putting their own lives and possessions at stake in the way of God—that their wholesome influence was not limited only to their age or the place where they fought their battles : they made even a deeper and lasting imprint on the successive generations of savants and reformers, or, rather, the entire Muslim community of Indo-Pak sub-continent. The struggle started by the Saiyid culminated into an armed resistance to the growing power of the British in India for the ultimate aim of the Saiyid's call was to save his country as well as the neighbouring Muslim states from the clutches of the new colonial power. The struggle was, for a long time, spearheaded by the religious scholars associated with the Saiyid's Movement. Similarly, the great effort made, during the nineteenth century, to translate and publish religious literature in the language spoken by the masses in order to bring the Islamic teachings within their reach owes its existence to the Saiyid's Movement. Of a fact, the religious and political awareness discernible among the Muslims in the recent past and the will to reassert their Islamic identity that followed their deep slumber in the days preceding, were brought about by this very Movement. For the Saiyid's Movement aimed at total religious and social transformation of the Muslims, it has left an indelible mark on their language and literature, thought and modes of expression.[1] Being a popular movement, its choice fell on Urdu, the language spoken by the people, for disseminating religious teachings through the spoken word and writings. Thus popularised, enriched and made capable of expressing deeper thoughts in a facile and graceful style, Urdu took the place of Persian which had earlier been the literary language of the country. The new Urdu idiom taking

1. Several Indian and Pakistani scholars have since written monographs and delivered lectures in Indian, British and American universities which trace the impact of the Jihād Movement of Saiyid Ahmad Shahīd and Ismā il Shahīd on the development of Urdu's idiom and style which has helped to make it a popular language. One such notable tract is Khwāja Ahmad Faruqi's *Urdū men Wahābi Adab*, published by the Delhi University in 1969.

shape under the impact of the Saiyid's Movement rejected the ornate and affected style of the earlier writers in favour of a fluent, vigorous and simple mode of expression and gave birth to a unique literary style in Urdu.

From Rae Bareli to Balakot

Tauhīd, or, oneness of Divine Being was the pivot of Saiyid's endeavour.[1] Worship is for God alone was his call and he raised it with such a courage and vehemence that his voice reverbated from every dale and hillock of India. Never before had this call been given with such vigour and force in this country. It invigorated the Muslims with a new spirit of faith and a burning zeal for fighting in the way of God. The Saiyid organised and trained the Muslims for the great venture he had in view and brought about a total transformation in their lives in accordance with the Islamic mould. On the 17th of Jamāda'l Ukhrā 1241 A. H. (1826) these soldiers of God arrived in the north-west corner of India (areas now included in the Peshawar and Mardan districts of Pakistan and independent tribal areas to make that place the centre of their activities. The Saiyid's objective was ot set up an independent, sovereign Islamic state in that part of the county and use it as the focal point for extending

---

1. *Sirāt-i-Mustaqīm* (Tr. 'Abdul Jabbār, Calcutta, 1856) by Saiyid Ahmad Shahīd and the *Taqwiyatul Imān* (Mujtabā'ī Press, Delhi, N. D.) by Shāh Ismā'īl Shahīd are the two invaluable books which fully explain the underlying thought of the Saiyid's revivalist Movement.

the Kingdom of God, based completly on the precepts of the Qur'ān and the *sunnah*, to the whole of India. He tried, on the one hand, to arouse Islamic spirit in the local population and, on the other, warned the tribal leaders and rulers of the surrounding Muslim principalities of the great danger hovering over their heads in the shape of rising British power in India which portended a threat to the very existence of Muslim power not merely in India but also to the neighbouring Muslim states and even to the Arab lands. He drew their atten-tion to the sneaky ways and the expansionist designs of the British, established contacts with the ruling chiefs in India as well as the rulers of Herat and Bukhāra, sent his envoys to them and repeatedly exhorted them through his episiles to wake up from their slumbering immobility. These letters exhibit the Saiyid's burning zeal for the welfare of the Muslims as well as his foresight, courage and vaulting ambition. If the sincerity and solicitude of the writer transpiring through these letters reflects the pure-hearted soul of the Saiyid, which is to be found in none except godly-minded reformers and religious teachers, the farsightedness shown by apprehending the impending danger and the judicious plan chalked out to meet that danger with unity, courage and fortitude show his unsurpassed qualities of leadership. Of a fact, the Saiyid surpassed his contemporaries in the qualities of head and heart. He was even ahead of the later-day politicians and statesmen, none of whom ever exhibited the signs of his prudence and foresightedness.

The call given by the Saiyid demanded re-introduction

of the observances and practices commended by the Qur'ān and the Prophet's *sunnah* in place of the then prevalent innovations and aberrations. He wanted to reinstate the *sharīah* in the Muslim Society for integrating the *ummah* with the whole of practical and conceptual structure of Islam. This allowed absolutely no place to anybody's personal interests, wishes and inclinations, political gains and worldly fame.[1]

The Saiyid had to traverse the forests and dales of Mālwā, the deserts of Rajasthān, Mewār and Sind and the hilly tracts of Buluchistān for reaching his destination in the north-west frontier of India. In the days when the modern means of transport did not exist, the journey involved terrible privations, scarcity of water, danger of attack by predatory bands, scaling of steep hills and encountering people whose language and customs were different from those of the wayfarers. The Saiyid and his followers had to cross the difficult Bolan Pass, the opening between jagged mountains separating Buluchistān from Afghānistān, cloven by nature perhaps for adventurers and conquerers. The road along the bed of Bolan river is in some places confined between steep

---

1. To be convinced of it one has to see the "Need of Jihād", in the fifth Chapter of the *Sirāt-i-Mustaqīm* and the letters written by Saiyid Ahmad Shahīd to the nobles and ruling chiefs of India, mystics, scholars and rulers of Afghānistān, Bukhāra and Turkistān. *Seerat Saiyid Ahmad Shahīd,* Vol, I, pp 384-95 and pp. 114-129 of *Saiyid Ahmad Shahīd—His Life and Mission* are also relevant to the issue.

precipices, while the hills on either sides are barren, dull and repulsive without any sign of life or vegetation. The narrow pass leads on to a still narrower and more steep Kozak Pass in Tauba Hills near Kandahar.

The royal welcome accorded to the Saiyid, in Kandahar, Ghaznī and Kabul was marked by huge enthusiasm of the local population. No ruler or religious leader had been so warmly received nor any one's visit had drawn such crowds on the roads and thoroughfares. It was as much an over-whelming manifestation of the people's fervour for their faith as it bespoke of the traditional hospitability of the Afghāns. Perhaps it was also indicative of their hopes and dreams as well as of their dissatisfaction with the existing conditions. They needed, in that phase of their national existence, a sincere leadership which could make them a united and disciplined people by shaking off the parochial regimes and family and tribal dictatorships imposed on them. They needed a leader who could rejuvenate their latent faculties which had, in days gone by, helped them to rise, time and again, as irresistible conquerors trampling the surrounding countries and shedding their blood in the defence of Islam.

The Saiyid visited Hashtnagar and Peshāwar where, too, the popular zeal to receive him with the greatest honour was as enormous as it had been at other places. After a brief stay at a Hashtnagar where he encouraged the Muslims to rise in defence of their faith, he moved on to Nowshehra. There he started giving a practical shape to *Jihad*, the great act of worship, for which he had undertaken the arduous journey and spent years in preaching, guiding and preparing the people. He sent an ultimatum to Ranjit Singh, from Nowshehra, offering him either to accept Islam or to pay the *Jizyah*, or, in the case of refusing both, to face him in the battle-field.[1]

The Saiyid was elected as *Amīr-ul-Mūminīn*[2] and he administered the oath of loyalty to his followers on the 12th of Jamādal, Ukhrā, 1242 A.H. (11th January, 1827). Friday sermon was recited in his name and a large number of tribal chiefs and religious scholars entered into his spiritual paternity, promising to abide by his orders and to fight in the way of God. They sent a joint memorandum to the ruler of Peshawar, who, finding his own chiefs and grandees in favour of accepting the Saiyid's leaderhip, bowed down to take the oath of allegiance to the Saiyid. Letters were thereafter despatched to the notable persons and religious leaders in India by Saiyid Ahmad Shahīd and Ismā'il Shahīd intimating them of the developments. The news was received with satisfaction and pleasure everywhere ; there was a consensus to support the Saiyid's efforts ; tribal leaders including the rulers of Peshawar Sardār Sultān Muhammad Khān and his brother Sardār Pir Muhammad Khān took the oath of allegiance to the Saiyid : and in the battle of Saidu about a

---

1. Muslim rulers had been, for centuries, overlooking this injunction of the *sharī'ah* in starting hostilities with the enemy.
2. *Lit.* Leader of the Faithful.

hundred thousand fighters of faith gathered round the banner of Saiyid Ahmad Shahīd.

The war with the government of Lahore was started strictly in accordance with Islamic injunctions following the precepts of the Prophet. The Sikhs, then ruling over the Punjab, held more or less a commanding position in the north-west frontier, there by threatening the independence of Afghanistan. They had, in fact, invaded that country several times. The Muslims of the Punjab, although in a majority and also rulers of the land since the fifth century of *Hijrah*, were being humiliated and harassed. An essential need of the time was to put an end to the tyranny they were undergoing and thus ward off the danger posed to the neighbouring Muslim States.

The Punjab had a great strategic importance. The war was declared against Ranjīt Singh[1] who was an ambitious and distinguished militarist and a powerful suzerain of the later part of the eighteenth century. Notwithstanding the huge military machine built up by Ranjīt Singh, the Saiyid's followers emerged successful in many a battle against powerful armies sent by Ranjīt Singh under the two experienced Italian Generals, Ventura and Allard, who had earlier served under Napoleon. The courage and valour, discipline and absolute submission to the *sharīah* injunctions, both in times

---

1. Ranjīt Singh (1780-1839) ruled over the territory extending from the banks of Jamuna in the south-east to Kabul in the north. For a fuller account of his exploits, see Sir Lepal Graffin's *Ranjīt Singh*.

of war and peace, exhibited by the Saiyid's troops were reminiscent of the pure-hearted followers of Islam in its earliest days.

The Saiyid established a truly Islamic State in the north-western regions including Peshawar. *Shari'ah* was enforced as the law of the State ; finance, administration, courts were all brought under the purview of the Islamic law. In-between the numerous Muslim kingdoms existing for centuries, which had been governed according to the whims of the rulers, more or less, as secular states, the state founded by the Saiyid was a living model of the *Khilāfat-i-Rāshidā*[1] of the earliest phase of Muslim rule.

But, alas, this blessed revolution was not to last for long and the events took the same course as had happened earlier time after time. Personal and tribal interests were whipped up and the defeated, crestfallen ignorance or the un-Islamic chauvinistic spirit threw its weight in favour of selfish instincts, reared and strengthened by the age-old customs of the tribal population, in order to wreak its vengeance upon Islam. Certain tribal chiefs headed by Sultān Muhammad Khān, the ruler of Peshawar, united to defy the Islamic authority. Although the latter had been given charge of Peshawar on his undertaking to enforce *shari'ah* as the law of the land—for this was the only reason for gaining control of Peshawar—the perfidious Khān conspired to do away with the functionaries of the Islamic government posted

---

1. *Lit.* The right-guided caliphate of the first four Caliphs of Islam.

in different areas. The massacre[1] was carried out so mercilessly that it would be difficult to find its parallel in the annals of revolts and revolutions. As it came to be known later on it was a deep-laid conspiracy in which all the tribal chiefs—those who were expected to act as *Ansārs*[2] to the *Mauhājirīn*[3]—had been involved. The incident, naturally, upset the entire system of the Islamic government. The Saiyid was forced to shift his head-quarters to another place and struggle anew for the establishment of the Islamic state. He, accordingly, went over to Hazara in Kashmir where he was promised full support and help by the tribal chiefs of the district in his great task.

The last encounter took place between the two sides at Balakot, a town perched in the hills in Kaghan valley, while Saiyid was on his way to Kashmir. Certain degenerate Muslims acted as spies of the enemy and guided Sher Singh, the son of Ranjīt, to mount an attack on the Muslim army. Here it was, in the last battle, that Saiyid Ahmad Shahīd, Ismā'īl Shahīd and a number of eminent and saintly leaders of the movement laid down their lives fighting like heroes. The encounter also witnessed many an ennobling examples of valour and bravery seldom seen in any battle. The disaster took place on 24th of Dhī Q'adā, 1246 A.H. (6th May, 1831).

---

1. About one hundred and fifty persons, all of whom were distinguished by their spiritual and moral qualities, are reported to have been put to death.
2. *Lit.* Helpers. The residents of Medina.
3. *Lit.* Emigrants from Mecca.

Mujāhidīn face the British

A little after the Saiyid's martyrdom, his followers established a stronghold of the Mujāhidīn in Sitana under the leadership of Wilāyat 'Ali and his brothers. They tried to emulate the Saiyid, but, by now, the enemy was not the Sikh Kingdom.[1] It had since been absorbed by the expanding British power which had by then gained a complete hold over the Indian sub-continent. This change was not unexpected; it was rather eminently in accord with the aim the Saiyid had set before himself from the very beginning of his Movement, as explicitly articulated by him in the letters he had written to ruling chiefs in India and Central Asia.

This renewed struggle for the defence of faith and freedom is a story of horrible trials and tribulations which makes one's hair stand on end even today. It was an unending process of attacks and assaults, senseless killing and destruction, confiscation of property, lengthy trials, official investigations, extradictions and sentences for death and life imprisonment which are reminiscent of the inquisitional tribunals of the Middle Ages. If all the sacrifices and deeds of valour performed during the struggle for India's freedom were to be put on one side of the balance and those of the house of Sadiqpur[2] in another; the latter would nodoubtedly prove to be more

---

1. Barely eighteen years after the death of Saiyid Ahmad Shahid, the British effaced the Sikh Kingdom out of existence in 1849.
2. Wilāyat Ali and his family belonging to 'Azimabad (Patna).

weighty.[1]

Amazing Organisation

An intricate net-work of the *Jihād* Movement was set up in India for the transfer of men, moneys and materials to the *mujāhidīn's* centre at Sitana. This secret organisation had several centres in Bihar and Bengal and elsewhere, too, which carried on correspondence in a secret code and trained volunteers who were sent out for taking part in the *Jihād* at a moment's notice ; not the greatest threat or inducement by the greatest empire of the day was successful in drawing away those associated with this movement.[2]

Ae unimaginable spirit of faith reinforced by selflessness and courage, willingness to die in the way of God and sacrificing zeal for Islam and unity among the Muslims was awakened by the Movement among the Bengali Muslims who were transformed into gallant combatants. Speaking about these people who have never had any militarist tradition, James O'kinealy, who had the charge of launching prosecutions in sedition and conspiracy cases, says, "The timid Bengali will, under certain conditions, fight as fiercely as an Afghan.[3]"

1. For details *see* Chapter 20-22 of *Saiyid Ahmad Shahīd—His Life and Mission* by Mohiuddin Ahmad, *Hindustān kī Pahlī Islāmī Tahrīk* by Mas'ūd 'Alam Nadwī and *Jamā't-i-Mujāhidīn* by Ghulām Rasūl Mehr.
2. *See* W. W. Hunter's ; *The Indian Musalmans* and Chapter 22 of *Saiyid Ahmad Shahīd—His Life and Mission.*
3. *Idid*, p. 150.

The people of Bengal had then become so strong in faith and firm in their Islamic behaviour that throughout the long spell of persecution faced by them, they never yielded ' to linguistic, cultural or racial chauvinism. They felt proud to be Muslims ; the criteria for merit recognised by them were the service of faith, propagation of Islam's message and virtuous behaviour.

The 'Alī Brothers of Sadiqpur had built up a marvellous system for organising the Muslims, reforming their faith and morals, enforcing the *shar'īa* laws among the communities joining the Movement and training the volunteers for *jihād*, and had succeeded in imparting the qualities of sincerity, sacrifice and a burning zeal for the service of Islam in their adherents. It would be no exaggeration to claim that India had not seen such a perfect organisation since the arrival of Muslims in this country up to 1864. A few excerpts given here from *'the Indian Musalmans'* by Sir William Hunter, one of the most inveterate enemies of the Saiyid's Movement will bear witness to this assertion.

''Indefatigable as missionaries, careless of themselves, blameless in their lives, supremely devoted to the over-throw of the British Infidels, admirably skilful in organising a permanent system for supplying money and recruits, the Patna Khalifs stand forth as the types and exemplars of the Sect.[1]''

X   X   X   X   X

''I find it impossible to speak of them without

1. Hunter, W. W., *The Indian Musalmans*, London, 1872, p. 68.

respect. Most of them start life as youths of ethu-siastic piety; many of them retain their zeal for religion to end, with singularly little tincture of the poisonous doctrines in which the Patna preachers have trained them......Certain it is that the Wahābī[1] Missionary furnishes, so far as my experience goes, the most spiritual and least selfish type of the sect.[2]"

X   X   X   X

"Yahyā 'Alī showed an admirable knowledge of character in selecting these men, for neither fear of detection nor hope of reward induced a single one of them to appear against their leader in the hour of his fall.[3]"

The movement had such a wide popularity that the British Government had to institute a special inquiry. Hunter, who has given the findings of this inquiry, says :

"The head of the Bengal Police reported that a single one of their preachers had gathered together some eighty thousand followers, who asserted complete equality among themselves, looked upon the cause of each as that of the whole sect, and considered nothing criminal, if done in behalf of a

---

1. The British nicknamed the movements as 'Wahābi' in order to bring it into discredit.
2. Hunter, W. W., *The Indian Musalmans*, p. 71
3. *Ibid.* p. 93

brother in distress.[1],,

The banner of revolt against the British raised, at last, in 1857 (popularly called Mutiny under the alian influence) was the handiwork of the left-overs of Mujāhidīn leaders[2] in India. Although the sister communities also joined in the rebellion, it did not succeed owing to a variety of reasons which cannot be discussed here. However, the leaders of the rebellion and particularly the Muslims had to bear the brunt of vindictive action taken by the British Government. Nothing that man can endure was spared to re-establish the authority of the alien Imperial power in India.[3]

The British government felt irritated by the armed resistance of the *Mujāhidīn* in the Frontier, the uprising in India and the criticism of its rule at home. It vent its anger on those Muslim nobles and religious scholars who were in any way connected with the *Mujāhidīn's* Centre at Sitana. Yahyā 'Ali of Azimabad, his brother Ahmad Ullah, his another relation 'Abdur Rahīm, Muhammad J'afar of Thanesar, Muhammad Shafī, a properous businessman of Lahore and several other

1. *Ibid*, p. 100 (cites letters No. 1001, dated 13th May, 1843, and No. 50 of 1847 from the Commissioner of Police, etc.).
2. It has been established beyond doubt that many of those who took a leading part in this freedom struggle like General Bakht Khān and Maulana Liāqat 'Alī had been closely associated with the Saiyid's Movement. Hunter also acknowledged that the left-over of the *Jihād* Movement had caused this conflagration.
3. For details *see* pp. 105-53 of the *Indian Muslimes, Lucknow,* by the Author.

persons were charged for waging war against the Queen in 1864. Yahyā 'Alī, 'Abdur Rahīm and Muhammad J'afar, along with a few other under-trials were lodged in Ambala Jail in separate solitary confinements and kept under inhuman conditions but their ecstatic happiness at their sufferings made the Englishmen marvel at their strong faith. Like the Prophet's companion, Khubayb, Yahyā 'Alī used to recite the verses the former had sung before being executed—

> I fear not which side I fall to depart ;
> It's all for God who will bless the limbs taken
> apart.

When, on 2nd May, 1864, the Sessions Judge, who was an Englishman, pronounced death sentence for Yahyā 'Alī, and said that he would be pleased to see him hanging on the gallows, Yahyā 'Alī felt so elated as if his heart' desire had been granted to him. Muhammad J'afar writes in the *Kālā Pānī*, "I still remember how pleased I was to hear the death sentence : I would not have felt more delighted if I had been made the ruler of seven Kingdoms." The strains of joy given out by the convicts were something beyond the understanding of those who have never tasted the fruit of faith. Perplexed and dismayed, the British Superintendent of Police, Captain Parson, who had felt a morbid pleasure in harassing and tormenting these poor souls, could not conceal his surprise and asked me, "You have been awarded death sentence. You ought to have shed tears but why are you so delighted ?" I replied, "In the hope of martyrdom which is the greatest blessing one can look for but you seem to know nothing of it."

All the convicts were lodged in Ambala Jail which drew crowds of English men and women who came to derive contentment from their distress. But the prisoners' blissful contentment left them all agog and whenever they asked the reason for the prisoners' cheerfulness, they got the same reply as was given to Captain Parson by Muhammad J'afar. When the British judges learnt that the prisoners welcomed the death sentence as the most befitting reward for their life-long efforts, they decided to deny the 'most treasonable among them the glory of martyrdom' as a measure of 'wise revenge',[1] On the 16th September, 1864, the Deputy Commissioner of Ambala, communicated the revised judgment of the Chief Court to the prisoners, saying, "Since you seem to relish the death sentence awarded to you and consider it to be martyrdom, the Government will not allow you to have punishment agreeable to you. Your death sentences have been commuted to transportation for life.[2]"

The prisoners were sent to Port Blair in the Andaman Islands in 1865 ; their house were demolished, the family graveyards were wiped out and their properies were confiscated. Yahyā 'Alī and Ahmad Ullah died serving the term of their imprisonment while Muhammad J'afar and 'Abdur Rahīm returned to India after serving

1. *The Indian Musalmans*, p. 98.
2. Muhammad Jafar, *Kālā Pānī* (also named as *Tawārikh-i-'Ajeeb*), Ambala, 1302 A. H.

(28)

18 years of their imprisonment in Andaman.[1]

The British rule continued till 1947 when the sub-continent ushered into era of freedom in the shape of two independent states, India and Pakistan. The territories forming part of Pakistan were the same where the Saiyid had launched his movement of reform and regeneration for the attainment of independence through *i'āhd*. But, there is a great difference in the position obtaining today and that visualised by the Saiyid. The aim he had before him, and for which he laid down his life were much more sublime and noble than the itical, administrative and social behaviour being witnessed today in that country.

Commendable Strategy

The skilful plan adopted by the Saiyid for achieving his political and military objectives was the best in the circumstances then prevailing. The strategy adopted by him bespeaks of his straight thinking, farsightedness and prudence. They can best appreciate its advantages who have studied, in depth, the political, social and military situation of the country in the beginning of the nineteenth century and are also aware of the attempts made earlier to achieve the ends he had in view. Several efforts had been made earlier by the ruling chief of Indian

---

1. For further details see *Kāla Pānī* (*Tawārikh 'Ajīb*) by Muhammad J'afar, Sufi Printing Press (Ambala, 1302 A. H.) and *Ad-Durr-el-Munsoor fi Tarājim Ahl-Sādiqpūr* by 'Abdur Rahim Zubairi (Patna, 1964).

States to rid the country of the imperialistic alien power and to create a strong and powerful political centre in the country, but each of these attempts had ended in failure. The foremost in this list were the ambitions sovereigns and brave generals like Tīpū Sultān (d.1214 A H./1799 A. D.) and Amir Khān (d. 1250 A. H. 1834 A. D.). Even earlier to them Nawāb Sirāj-ud-Daula of Murshidabad (d. 1170 A. H./1757 A.D.) and Nawab Shuj'ā-ud-Dawla of Oudh (d. 1177 A. H /1764 A. D.) had failed to make any headway in spite of their vast resources and military strength. The reason for their failure was, first, the policy of divide and rule pursued by the Englishmen and, secondly there was no territory left in India which was completely free from the British influence where preparation to wage war against them could be made undisturbed and with complete freedom of action.

Needless to say that such plans for military operations are adopted after giving careful thought to the best alternative and discussions with military advisers. If such a leader happens to have the pleasure of God also in his view, he takes recourse to prayers and supplications to the Lord with a humble heart and, then, places his reliance on the help of God. Now, turning to the Saiyid, we find him fulfilling all these conditions without the least neglience in any matter.

Now, to bring in our own standards and present-day values in pronouncing a judgement on any individual or movement of the times past, whose circumstances and methods were different from ours, is unjustified or rather unrealistic. It is more so if the efforts of which we form an estimate did not lack sincerity and diligence, for verily, the outcome always depends on the will of Providence. If we were to adopt success or failure as the sole criterion for estimation of any effort, we would have to give up many an enchanting and shining example of ennobling sacrifice and service of faith in the history of Islam. For the merit of any deed in Islam lies in the sincerity of purpose, noble intention, relentless effort and devotion to the cause and not in the resultant upshot, material benefits and apparent accomplishments. The Qur'ān is quite explicit on this point.

"Of the believers are men who are true to that which they covenanted with Allah. Some of them have paid their vow by death (in battle), and some of them still are waiting ; and they have not altered in the least."[1]

Commenting on the Saiyid's Movement and the struggle taking its rise from it, Ghulām Rasūl Mehr has correctly stated that :

"It is a chapter of the history of Indo-Pak sub-continent, pertaining to the period known as the era of decadence, but can any just and truthful man deny the fact that there is hardly any event of the days when Islam was triumphant and topping, which is more illustrious, more dignified than it ? The worth of any deed depends not on its result or outcome but on the resolute will, courage and perseverence with which the aim is pursued,

1. Q. XXXIII : 23.

(31)

Can anyboby claim that there are similar examples of equal tenacity and gallantry even in the days when we were in the ascendant, wherein the sole objective was, like it, nothing but the service of faith?,,[1]

Revolutionary Reforms

One of the greatest achievements of Saiyid Ahmad Shahīd was that he revived *jihād*, a fundamental teaching of Islam, which had been given up, with the passage of time, as impracticable and no more binding on the Muslims. Its traces were then found only in the Qur'ān and the *hadīth* and the biographies of the earliest followers of Islam who had waged war for the sake of God and glorification of His Word. They had fought with the least concern for their own selves and their families and were indifferent to personal benefits or advantages to be gained or even the consolidation of their authority through their conquests. The Muslim kings had more often utilised the fervour of *jihād*, for their personal ends and deliberately neglected its aims and injunctions. On the other hand, those engaged in the propagation or faith and morals were either too pre-occupied in their task or lacked the capacity to revive it. And, thus the Muslims had gradually forgotten the importance of *jihād*, assigning it a place even lower to certain minor

---

1. Ghulām Rasūl Mehr, *Saiyid Ahmad Shahid*, (Lahore 1952), Vol. I, p. 16.

(32)

issues[1] of *fiqah*[2], and relegated it to the category of acts viewed as simply desirable by the *sharī'ah*.

Indifference to this essential obligation enjoined by Islam did a great harm to the Muslims : unworthy and evil-minded persons lacking conscience and fear of God were emboldened ; dignity of Islam and the Muslims suffered a set-back ; and, the Muslims who had for several hundred years wielded the sceptre became weak and despised in their own country. Their mosques were demolished, the Muslims were humbled and humiliated and this foreboding of the Prophet of Islam stared them in the face.

"When you will give up *jihad*, Allah will deliver you to disgrace and will not remove it until you return to your faith.[3]"

The entire world of Islam, particularly the regions lying far away from the centre of Uthmānī Caliphate, had been subjected to this humiliation.

The Saiyid has himself explained the necessity and importance of *jihād* in the *Sirāt-i-Mustaqīm*, in these words.

"Have a look at Rūm and Turkey and compare

---

1. Maulānā Ismā'il Shahīd, who was the closest associate of the Saiyid, or rather his spokesman, writes in a letter to the scholars : "The religious scholars do not nowadays attach even as much importance to *jihād* as they do to the juristic injunctions relating to mensuration and purity from it.
2. Islamic Jurisprudence
3. Abū Daū'd on the authority of Ibn 'Umar

the present state of this country in the year 1233 A.H. (A.D. 1818) when the greater portion of it has become the country of the enemy *(Dār-ul-harb)*, with the conditions prevailing some two or three hundred years back, and contrast the blessings of Heaven now vouchsafed, and the number of saints and learned men with those of that period.[1]"

The Saiyid's *jihād* revived this forgotten obligatory duty lying on the Muslim. He waged it not only in its original shape and form, but he also brought about a tremendous change in the aptitudes and inclinations, way of thinking and literary compositions[2] of the Indian Muslims. Fear of death fled away from the hearts, courting of hardships in the way of God became a child's play and martyrdom became the spur that made men struggle with destiny. Numerous youngmen of well-to-do families gave up their lives of ease and comfort;

---

1. Saiyid Ahmad Shahīd, *Sirāt-i-Mustaqīm*, (ed. Shah Mohammad Ismail, tr. 'Abdul Jabbār) pp. 318-19, Calcutta, 1856.

2. Momin Khān Momin's poems extrolling *Jihād* and the *Qasida-i-jihādiyah* by Khurram 'Ali provide an irrefutable evidence to the new trend of thought and its expression in literary compositions. These poems were recited in front of the troops arranged in the battle-field. Saiyid 'Abdur Razzaq Kalāmī, a relation of the Saiyid, had poetized Islamic history under the name of '*Futhūh-us-Shām* or *Samsām-ul-Islām*' (published by Newal Kishore Press, Lucknow) which comprised twenty-five thousand verses. It became extremely popular all over the country. All this was brought about by the Saiyid's movement of *jihād*.

started living as mendicants willing to undergo all hardships in order to prepare themselves for migration and *jihād*. The yearning to take part in *jihād* so powerfully captured the imagination of the masses that women started singing such lullabies to lull their children to sleep—

Oh Lord, let me a martyr be,
Greatest of the great homage to Thee.

The people were so carried away by the enthusiasm for *jihād* and martyrdom that not unoften a father presented his own son for enlistment in the *Mujāhīdīn* force. Nawāb Farzand 'Alī of Ghazipur brought his son to the Saiyid saying, "I wish that he were slain like Ismā'il." Youngmen used to cast lots for going away to take part in the *jihād* and those who showed sluggishness were admonished by their parents. Writing about the then prevailing hurricane of enthusiasm for *jihād* writes W. W. Hunter.

"No Wahabi father who has a boy of more than usual parts or piety, can tell the moment at which his son may not suddenly disappear from the hamlet.[1]"

The Saiyid's another great achievements was revival of *Imāmat*, an essential part of Islamic polity, given up by the Muslims since a long time. The result was that they had become a disorganised mob, having no central authority either to guide or guard their interest. Islam looks with horror at this state of affairs and considers it

---

1. W. W. Hunter, *The Indian Musalmans*, p. 112.

as nothing less than paganism. It warns the Muslims that they should neither live nor die without an *Imām* or rightly-guided leader. This great *sunnah* of the Prophet, which is also an obligatory duty lying on every Muslim, was restored by the Saiyid at a time when the followers of Islam in most of the countries had abandoned it since long.

It would have been sufficient to win the hearts of Muslims as a worthy reformer if the Saiyid had done nothing more than the restoration of these two decidedly essential but long forgotten precepts of Islam, but there are many more services rendered by him which place him in the list of unforgettable personages of Islamic history. One of these was renewal of the vanishing practice of going for the *haj* pilgrimage. The scholars of India had, in his time, hit upon many a legal and plausible excuse[1] for not undertaking the journey on account of lawlessness and hazards of sea voyage. At this stage, one might recall the speech delivered by the Saiyid at Balamau in District Rae Bareli before he set out for *haj* in 1236 A. H., which depicts gravity of the situation and his heartache at it.

"I have been constantly praying God for my countrymen: 'O God, the way to Thy K'aba has been blocked. Thousands of moneyed men who paid *zakat*, have died under the self-delusion or were misled by the devil that the voyage is not safe.

1. *Saiyid Ahmad Shahid—His Life and Mission*, pp. 207-211 and 319-20.

Thousands of the wealthy are still there who do not undertake the journey because of this fear. Make the journey so easy, My Lord, that whoever wants to go for the *haj*, may not be denied this great blessing. My prayer has been answered by the Lord who has promised to allow no impediments to remain after I return from this *haj*. All those brothers who will remain alive, will see for themselves the truth of what I say.[1]"

Similarly, the remarriage of widows was looked down upon as an affront to the family honour in those days. Any one who dared to break this convention, had to face a social boycott by his friends and relatives. This custom had been taken over by the noble and well-to-do families of the Muslims from the Hindus during the last days of Mughal Rule in India and had become so deeply-rooted that certain doctors of law had even issued juristic opinions against the remarriage of widows.[2] The Saiyid put an end to this pernicious taboo which gave a new life to thousands of his unfortunate sisters. By re-establishing this practice among the India Muslims, he revived a *sunnah* and a command of the *sharīat* besides bringing about a social reform in the Indian Muslim society.

Late marriage of girls was an established practice among the Afghāns, which, too, was given up through the efforts of Saiyid Ahmad Shahīd. This abnormality had

1. *Sirat Saiyid Ahmad Shahīd*, Vol. 1, p. 262
2. *Saiyid Ahmad Shahīd—His Life and Mission*, pp, 75-76

given birth to numerous physical, social and moral evils. Similarly, there were numerous other social usages accepted by the Muslims of India owing to their general ignorance of the Islamic teachings or were borrowed from their Hindu neighbours. These conventions and customs were very often opposed to Islamic behaviour and morals or fell in the category of innovations and aberrations popularised by the misguided sects among Muslims. A large number of these were either given up or reformed under the salutary influence of the Saiyid. This is not all ; the Islamic state founded by the Saiyid enforced the *Shar'īat* in its totality—financial. revenue, civil and criminal administration was, patterned strictly according to Islamic Law ; *Cadīs* and *Muhtasibs* were appointed ; attention was paid to the promulgation of what was right and prohibition of what was evil ; and steps were taken for the dissemination of the message of Islam. In short, the Saiyid held up to the view of the world, when it had lost sight of it, a true model of Islamic state and society as it existed during its earliest phase.[1]

And, a still greater achievement was the revolutionary change brought about by the Saiyid in the Indian Muslim society. His preachings and reformatory endeavours had created an atmosphere of spirituality and piety while his devoted disciples took his message from house to house in every nook and corner of the country. Attitudes

1. *Saiyid Ahmad Shahīd—His Life and Mission*, pp. 207-211 and 319-320.

and inclinations were changed : propinquity to God instead of worldly objects became the ultimate aim of endeavour of every hand. A new reformative movement, religious and educational in its make up, emerged and enveloped the whole of India.

It would not be out of place to cite a few instances of the change in the general atmosphere. While the Saiyid was staying at Calcutta on his way to the *haj* pilgrimage the sale of wine dwindled to such an extent that the liquor dealors preferred a petition to the East India Company's government that the tax on its sale should be remitted. They stated in their petition that from the day a religious-minded men had arrived in the city with his followers, the Muslims of the town and rural areas were taking oaths of fidelity at his hand, promising to desist from the drinking of the liquor and other evils with the result that the wine shops were giving a deserted look. Thousands of persons who had concubines, according to the prevalent custom, either married them or severed their illegal connections. Muslim ladies took to the observance of *purdah*, un-Islamic practices were given up and the observances commended by Islam were adopted. A new life was infused in the missionary endeavours resulting into innumerable conversions to Islam in Bengal and Assam.[1] This did not happen in Calcutta alone, it became the praxis of the entire country.

---

1. *Saiyid Ahmad Shahid—His Life and Mission*, pp. 86-88

Comprehensive and Far-reaching Effects

The Saiyid's Movement exercised an all-embracing and extensive influence on the Muslims of India. The call given by him for purification of morals, restoration the matrix of *sharī'ah*, revival of the Quranic commands and prophetic practices and glorification of the Word of God gave rise to numerous religious, social and educational movements which generated a new awakening among the Muslims. The reformative movement of Nisār 'Ali (Titū Miān) in East Bengal, the *Ahl-Hadīth* (followers of Traditions) movement having its centres all over the country, Sadiqpur's recruitment and training centre for *jihād.* the missionary endeavours of the Ghaznavī family of Amritsar, the two Dār-ul-ulooms of Saharanpur and Deoband with a net-work of institutions for religious education and, finally, the Nadwatul 'Ulama's centre of higher education—all these and many others have grown out of the seeds sown by the Saiyid. They were all illuminated by the light emitted by him as a poet has said :

> From the only candle of this abode. such
> shadows are cast,
> Wherever my eyes fall, a fraternity I spot.

Hostile attitude of the Orientalists

The Saiyid's comprehensive programme for regeneration of the Muslim society was unique among the revivalist movement in Islam started during the preceding centuries. Also, there are few reformers who won the admiration of their contemporaries and the coming generations like him. Still, of all the worthies of the world, excepting, of course, the blessed Prophet of Islam, no man has ever been so maligned by the Western writers and historians as was the Saiyid.[1]

It seems that the chroniclers never wanted to ascertain true facts : they gave credence to every groundless rumour without evaluating the relative evidential value of the reports reaching them. The emphasis on freedom of thought, rejection of irrational beliefs and inclinations accepted earlier without investigation of the truth were the great gifts of European renaissance. The conflicts steeped in blood between the traditional beliefs and the expansive force of human intellect had drawn on a daybreak of intellectual curiosity which had benefited not only the West but the entire humanity. It was. therefore, expected that the orientalists and historians of the later half of the last and present century would at least prove themselves to be more enquiring and broadminded than their predecessors who had been brought up under the shadow of narrow-spirited uncharitableness

1. Some might think that the great Arabian reformer, Sheikh 'Abdul Wahhāb (1115-1206 A H.) was equally or perhaps more maligned than the Saiyid. It is, however, noteworthy that whatever accounts exist relating to Sheikh 'Abdul Wahhāb, they are mostly the writings of Muslims themselves in Arabic, Turkish and other eastern languages and no campaign to stigmatize him was ever launched by the Western scholars. The Saiyid's case differs from others inasmuch as that we do not find any parallel attempt to discredit anyone like him.

bequeathed by the Crusades, and for whom it was difficult, if not impossible, to deliver themselves from the mental climate of that Age. But, man is a bundle of contradictory complexes, for one often comes across examples of human behaviour least expected of the persons professing to be rationalists.

A Known Figure : Reliable Chronicles

Saiyid Ahmad Shahīd was not a legendary figure taken out of the pages of the Arabian Nights. He was born and brought up during the closing decades of the eighteenth century in that part of northern India which was the cultural centre of Muslim India, and was later known as the United Provinces of Agra and Oudh. Saiyid Ahmad Shahīd was the descendant of a well-known Saiyid family of Oudh which enjoyed the esteem of its coreligionists because of a number of saintly figures born in that family during the past five hundred years. Their nobility of blood, temperance, ascetic selflessness and zeal for religion had made even the Moghul Emperors render honour to them. Not a few Persian chronicles written during the period possess irrefragable evidence about the services of this family. The Saiyid first established contact with the famous family of Shāh Walīullāh which had held aloft the banner of reform and regeneration of Indian Islam. Thereafter, he joined the army of Amīr Khān, the well-known ambitious Afghān hailing from Sambhal in Uttar Pradesh. The dutiful regard and devotion bestowed by Amīr Khān on the Saiyid is no secret, nor is the life of this Afghān chief an enigma. Several works exist about him which show how very different was he from the Pindāris with whom he is so often equated.

After the end of his sojourn with Amīr Khān, began the period of Saiyid's reformatory endeavour during which he stirred a hurricane of religious enthusiasm and zeal for moral uprightness and piety, not among the masses alone, but also in the learned and nobility of the country. During his missionary tours in the then North-Western Province and Oudh, people flocked round him in thousands, in a way unheard of in the country earlier, to take the oath of allegiance to him. They repented of their past sins and solemnly promised to give up all un-Islamic customs and practices and to betake the path of virtue and goodness.[1]

The Saiyid then undertook the journey for pilgrimage to Mecca with a retinue of about seven hundred and fifty persons. This triumphal pilgrims' progress of the Saiyid, inconceivable in those days, was a feat unsurpassable by any sovereign or religious leader of the time. From his home town of Rae Bareli to Calcutta, he sowed the seeds of righteouness and moral and spiritual betterment. All along the route through which his caravan moved, the people in cities after cities enrolled themselves as his disciples and undertook to carry on his message of social reform and moral uplift.[2]

1. *Saiyid Ahmad Shahīd—His Life and Mission*, pp. 59-77.
2. *Ibid.*, pp. 79-88

The reverential regard and honour extended to the Saiyid in Mecca was unique for any non-Arab religious leader for none had been held in such a high esteem for a long time in that metropolis of Islam. This was the time when Wahābī power had been completely shattered in Arabia and nobody could dare preach its doctrines without putting himself into peril. No documentary evidence or authoritative proof exists of the Saiyid's coming into contact with any Wahābī preacher. Far from being treated as a heretic, the collection of his discourses, *Sirāt-i-Mustaqīm*, was rendered into Arabic on the request of the religious scholars of Mecca. The Saiyid had, in fact, already finalised the blueprints of his socio-religious reforms before undertaking the journey for *haj* and unfolded its practical details, based on his own understanding of the Qur'ān and the *sunnah*, during his reformatory tours in India.[1]

On his return from *haj*, the Saiyid gave a practical shape to his concept of *khilāfat* which could unite the whole of the Muslim world from India to Central Asia and Turkey for the service of Islam. Nothing that Saiyid did was not premeditated. He chose the hilly tract of independent tribesmen in the Frontier for lunching the *jihād*, for which he had to traverse a vast tract of mountainous countries and deserts over Sind, Baluchistan and Afghanistan. Records of his itinerary give the details of his every stopover and the distances covered as well as the social customs and habits of the people

1. *Saiyid Ahmad Shahid-His Life and Mission, op. cit.,* pp. 98-109.

along his route more or less in the same manner as can be expected of an official diary of an escort of armed forces moving in the modern times. The Saiyid maintained contact with the missionary centres in India, sent circular letters to the *ulāmā* and religious leaders from time to time and got the happenings in the Frontier recorded by his amanuenses. Several collections of these writings are to be found in different libraries and private collections in India as well as in the British Museum.

The arrangement made for recording the events pertaining to the Saiyid's life, after his martyrdom in May 1831 at Balakot, were also unprecedented. A few of these deserve to be mentioned. The First one is the voluminous account compiled at the instance of Nawāb Wazīr-ud-daulā, the ruler of Tonk, who called upon the associates and comrades of the Saiyid to reduce into writing their reminiscences and experiences with him. This was thus the first eye-witness record of the Saiyid's life story. Compiled in four bulky volumes, this is known by the name of *Waqāi Ahmadī* of which several copies exist at different places.[1] The second biography of Saiyid Ahmad Shahīd was written under the title of *Manzooratus So ada fī Ahwāl il-Ghozāt was-Shuhadā'* by Saiyid J'afar 'Alī Naqvī (d. 1288 A. H.), a Persian scholar of distinction belonging to a reputed family of the Saiyids of Gorakhpur. Saiyid J'afar 'Alī Naqvī had not only participated in the Frontier campaigns of the

---

1. A manuscript of the book is also preserved in the Nadwatul 'Ulama Library.

Saiyid but was also his official correspondent. Thus, he had the unique opportunity of obtaining first-hand information of all the happenings and events in the Frontier.

The third biographical account of the Saiyid was from the pen of Saiyid's eldest nephew, Saiyid Muhammad 'Alī (d. 1266 A. H.). This monograph in Persian, named *Makhzan-i-Ahmadī*, is the most reliable source for the Saiyid's biographical accounts from his birth up to his return from the *haj* as the author had been the closest companion of the Saiyid, besides being closely related to him. It was written when Nawāb Muhammad 'Alī Khān ruled over Tonk and was published from Agra in 1882.

The fourth authentic source is the *Sawāneh Ahmadī* by Muhammad J'afar of Thanesar who was one of the accused in famous conspiracy case of 1864. This was the first biography written in Urdu and was popularly received. The author, bound by an oath of allegiance to the Saiyid's spiritual successors, was his devoted follower and had also undergone the sentence for deportation for a period of 18 years, but it was written at the time when the alien rulers of India were allergic of everything even remotely connected with the Saiyid and his movement. Muhammad J'afar's pen had thus to be cautious and could not disclose many facts that required freedom of expression.

Then, a very comprehensive biography entitled *Saiyid Ahmad Shahīd* was penned in four volumes covering 1921 pages by Ghulām Rasūl Mehr. The book, published from Lahore between 1952 to 1956, is really encyclopaedic in its scope and content in so far as the events relating to the Saiyid and his close companions are concerned.

The writer of these lines had also attempted a biography which was first brought out in 1939 under the name of *Sirat Saiyid Ahmad Shahīd* with an enchanting introduction by the great scholar Syed Sulaimān Nadwi. Being the first literary endeavour of the writer when he was only 24 years of age, this monograph of modest size covered 462 pages. But, the way this work was received was a sure indication of the popularity of Saiyid Ahmad Shahīd and the urge of the people to know more about him. Political situation then obtaining in the country had again created an upsurge in the Muslims who were eager to re-assert their identity and to see Islam strong and powerful in the world. Naturally, the Saiyid's message of hope and faith, of self-confidence and self-realization, contained in the book, was enthusiastically welcomed by them. Several editions of it were brought out one after another in which the writer went on making additions and improvements till it was published for the fifth time from Pakistan in 1974. Its sixth reprint, comprising two volume and covering 1445 pages with several maps and pictures of historical places was brought out from Lucknow in 1978.

Finally there is the *Saiyid Ahmad Shahīd—His Life and Mission*, written in English by Mohiuddin Ahmad, which is the result of a deep study and research according to the modern critical approach. It takes note of a large number official reports and historical records of the period. The book containing 440 pages has been hailed as the most definitive work on Saiyid Ahmad Shahīd In addition to the works mentioned here, there are several other studies, articles and monographs appearing from time to time in India and Pakistan and even in the Western countries.

Unfortunately, there is little to be found on the subject in Arabic with the result that the Arabic speaking world is generally unacquainted with this great reformer and his achievements. The first attempt in this direction was, perhaps, made by this writer whose article on the Saiyid was published by late Syed Rashīd Raza, first in his reputed Journal *Almanār* during 1349-50 A. H. (A. D. 1931) and then in the shape of a brochure. The article captioned as *As-Saiyid al-Imām Ahmad ibn Irfān as Shahīd Mujaddid al-Qarn al-Thālith ʻUshr* was written at the age of 17 years and hence, it lacked the maturity of thought and expression expected from an experienced writer, but the defect was compensated by another work of modest size in Arabic, *Izā Habbat Rīh-ul-Imān*, as this second work was named, which gave an account of the back-ground of Saiyid's Movement and its achievements. It has since been published thrice from Lucknow and Beirut.

Everything about Saiyid Ahmad Shahīd, from his birth to death is, thus, in the light of the day. Only he can plead ignorance of all this material who has wilfully decided to shut his eyes to these factual details. To be

(48)

content to take Saiyid Ahmad Shahīd as portrayed in the fabricated chronicles of certain inimical writers, despite all this copious and trustworthy details satisfying the modern criteria of historical criticism, is perhaps an intriguing phenomenon of modern scholarship.

A few examples of Animosity to the Saiyid

A few examples of irresponsible allegations made by some of our Western scholars, who are otherwise too meticulous in putting everything on the grill, are given here to show their deep-rooted animosity to the Saiyid.

A reputed orientalist of the nineteenth century, Thomas Patrick Hughes, writes in his article on "Wahhabi" in the *Dictionary of Islam* :

> "And so it came to pass that when a restless spirit from India was endeavouring to redeem a lawless life by performing the pilgrimage at Makkah, he fell in with teachers who had imbibed Wahhabi doctrines and were secretly disseminating them amongst the pilgrims. Saiyid Ahmad, the free-booter and bandit having performed the sacred rites of the Pilgrimage, returned from Makkah (A. D. 1822), resolved to reclaim the whole of North India to the Faith of Islam.[1]"

Modern scholarship is not very different in its rancorous attitude to the Saiyid. Olaf Caroe, who had been the Governor of North West Frontier Province during the last two years before the transfer of power in

---

1. *Dictionary of Islam*, London, 1865, p. 661

(49)

1947, is on record in his scholarly book entitled *The Pathans* :

"Saiyid Ahmad Barelvi had been the follower of the notorious Amīr Khān, a leader of the mercenaries in the campaigns waged by the British against the free-booters of Central India known as Pindāris. He lost his employment when Amīr Khān's force was broken up at the end of the campaign, and Amīr Khān was recognised as Chief of Tonk in Rajputana.[1]"

In a recent monograph entitled *"The Muslims of British India"*, Dr. P. Hardy present his research in these words :

"Saiyid Ahmad was born into an obscure family, possibly in minor official service.........From about 1809 to 1818, he was a trooper under the Pindari chieftain Amīr Khān, later the *nawwāb* of Tonk ; probably there was nothing to distinguish him outwardly from other Pindari freebooters.[2]"

Similarly, W. W. Hunter, who had the greatest opportunity of ascertaining facts from the Saiyid's followers and might have very well known them, says in the *Indian Musalmans* :

"Syed Ahmad was publicly degraded and expelled from the town (Mecca).[3]

1. *The Pathans*, London, 1965, p. 301
2. *The Muslims of British India*, Cambridge, 1972, p. 52.
3. *The Indian Musalmans*, pp. 60-61.

Again he writes :

"In 1822, he made a religious journey to Mecca ; and having thus completely covered his former character as a robber beneath the sacred garb of a pilgrim, he returned in October of the following year by Bombay.[1]"

These are the few examples of Western scholarship which bear witness to its capricious ways in dealing with certain matters not to its liking. This was least expected from European scholars who are otherwise thoroughly proficient in the collation and critical examination of the relative evidential value of historical data.

Eastern followers of the Orientalists

Chroniclers of the Orient, particularly these belonging to Middle Eastern countries, who have had an occasion to pen treatises on Wahābī, Mahadawī and *Jihād* movements of India have also not fared better than their European counterparts. They, too, have been content to repeat the reports which were neither faithful nor complete as regards the Saiyid's movement of *jihād*. This is strange as well as painful for they could have easily ascertained the facts from the Indian scholars or the centres of Arabic learning and education in India, if they did not possess a direct access to the original sources. The scholars of the Arab world are also aware how inimical, partisan attitudes and political interests had run down Sheikh 'Abdul Wahhāb, the great reformer of the

---

1. *The Indian Musalmans, op, cit.,* p. 13.

twelfth century of Islamic era. and reflected discredit upon him. The Arab scholars are not unoften seen protesting against such vilifying attempts. But, strangely enough, they, too, are guilty of the same error. To give an example of it, we give an extract from the *As-Sheikh Muhammad bin Abdul Wahhāb*, written by Ahmad b. Hajr b. Muhammad, a Cādī of Qatar, which has been published for wide circulation by the government of Saudi Arabia.

"It was in this manner that the call of Sheikh Muhammad 'Abdul Wahhāb influenced certain parts of India. This came about through the efforts of an Indian Hājī Saiyid Ahmad who was one of the ruling chiefs of the country. Having accepted Islam[1] in 1816, he undertook the journey to Hijaz for performing the *haj* where he met the Wahhābīs. He was convinced that the call of Sheikh 'Abdul Wahhāb was perfectly bassed on the teachings of Islam and thus he became an ardent supporter of Wahhabism.[2]"

This is, in fact, an inevitable result of accepting the statements of orientalists without any scrutiny. The same has been the case with the reputed Egyptian scholar and penman, Dr, Ahmad Amīn, who has written brilliant dissertions entitled *Fajr al-Islām. Dhuh-al Islām* and *Zuhr*

---

1. It is amusing to see that the writer uses the prefix "Saiyid" with the name of Saiyid Ahmad Shahid, but it did not strike him that a Saiyid could never be a new convert to Islam.
2. *As-Sheikh Muhammad b. 'Abdul Wahhāb*, Mecca, 1395 A. H., p. 78.

al-Islām on the subject of Islamic history, but he has, unfortunately, completely relied on the peccant reports of English and French orientalists in regard to the Saiyid and his endeavours in *Al-Mahdawiato-wal-Mahdiyūn*. In *Zu'ama-il-Islāh fil'Asr-il-Hadīth* he writes in the section giving an account of Sheikh Muhammad Abdul Wahhād.

"A Wahhābī leader and reformer, named Saiyid Ahmad, was born in India. He performed *haj* in 1822 and then held aloft the banner of Wahhābī message in the Punjab where he established his authority. His power coutinued to grow until it posed a threat to the Northern India. He contended not only against innovations and aberrations but also drew his sword against preachers and religious scholars of the area. He fought against all those who refused to accept his call and mission, and declared India to be *Dar-ul harb*. The British and their allies had to face considerable difficulty in curbing his power but they ultimately succeeded in completely suppressing him.[1]"

This brief account by Ahmad Amīn contains as many mistakes as the lines it covers, and they are so blatantly wrong that it would even be futile to discuss them. Anyone who is even superficially aware of the Saiyid's life, his reformative movement and his *jihād* or the history of that period will know that every single fact

---

1. *Zum'a-il-Islah fi 'Asr-il-Hadīth*, p. 21

stated by Ahmad Amīn is incorrect. The reason for committing such a grievous mistake is that he blindly depended on the orientalists and did not consider it necessary to gather the information through his own study or even ask about it from those who were well-versed in the history of Indian Muslims and very often visited Egypt also. Had he done so, he would have accorded the foremost place among the reformers of India to the Saiyid instead of Sir Syed Ahmad Khān and Syed Amīr Alī. During my visit to Egypt in 1951, when I drew his attention to his mistakes and told him about the achievements of the Saiyid and Shāh Ismā'īl Shahīd, he readilly acknowledged that he did not possess adequate information about the two nor he knew about the great influence exercised by them on the Muslim society and Islamic thought in India.[1]

Opinion of Contemporary Scholars

The worth of a man can best be judged from the estimations of his contemporary men of letters. It would, therefore, be worthwhile to reproduce a few of these here.

The well-known historian and scholar, Nawāb Syed Siddīq Hasan Khān of Bhopāl (d. 1307 A.H.) who was himself a witness to the influence wielded by the Saiyid's movement writes in the *Tiqsār-o-Juyūd-il-Ahrār*.

"A sign of God was he in guiding the people

1. For a fuller report see the author's *Sharq Ausat Kī Diary*, Lucknow, 1977, pp. 51-52.

on the right path and making their hearts incline towards God. A large number of people became pure-hearted saints through the potent influence exerted by him, while his spiritual successors swept-ed the country clean of all innovations and polytheis-tic thoughts and practices and made the masses betake the path of the Book and the *sunnah.* The blessings of his noble efforts are still visible. ....In short, there was none so godly and perfect of spiril in the whole world in those days, nor was there any mystic or religious scholar who exerted such a salutary influence even over one-tenth of the people as he did.[1]"

Hyder 'Alī of Rampur, a savant among scholars, had the honour of being taught by Shāh 'Abdul 'Azīz, the reputed son of Shāh Wāliullah. He writes in Siyānat-un-Nās 'An Waswasatal Khannās.

"Tne light of his guidance rose like the glorious lamp of heaven and illuminated of all the lands and hearts of the people. Thousands of persons who had been long accustomed to polytheistic practices, repented of their sins and betook the right path, of the Book and the *sunnah.* His spiritual disciples travelled from land to land showing the path of righteousness to innumerable persons.

"The Saiyid appointed thousands of his spiritual successor who continue to administer oath of allegiance to the people and guide them through

---

1. *Tiqsār·o-Juyūd-il-Ahrār,* Bhopal, 1298, A. H., pp. 109-110.

their sermons. There were persons who detested prayer and fasting; revelled in drinking spree; indulged in adultery, illegal gratification, usury and misdemeanour; disputed the need of *haj* and *zakāt*, and shamelessly jested with the *sharī'at* saying that neither the prayer was commended by the Company nor fast was prescribed by the Council. It was through the teachings of the Saiyid that such persons repented from their sinful ways, contracted legal marriages, got themselves circumcised and became virtuous and pious. As many as ten thousand persons often took the oath at his hand, in a single day, while a large number of Hindūs, Shī'ās and Yogis accepted Islam by listening to his sermons. Even Christians used to approach him secretly to embrace his faith. Innumerable religious scholars engaged themselves in providing guidance to the populace after taking the *bi·at* from him; some of them wrote commentaries on the Quranic verses and Traditions; published books and tracts in the language understood by the masses for imparting knowledge of religion to those who were earlier ignorant even about the creed (*kalimah*) of the Muslims.[1]"

'Abdul Ahad was another scholar who had met and conversed with a number of disciples of the Saiyid.

---

1. Hyder 'Ali Rāmpūri, *Siyānat-un-Nās 'An Waswastal Khannas*, 1270 A. H, pp. 4-6.

He testifies that :

"About forty thousand Hindus and other non-Muslims were converted to Islam by the Saiyid while thirty hundred thousand Muslims had pledged fidelity, to him. The number of those who took the oath on the hands of Saiyid's disciples and their spiritual successors exceeds tens of millions.[1]"

Wilāyat 'Alī[2] of 'Azīmābād (d. 1269 A. H.), a prominent disciple of the Saiyid, who also took part in the *jihād* writes :

"As soon as the Saiyid gave his call of religious reform, people from every part of the country gathered round him. His popularity rose to the extent that oftentimes crowds consisting of as many as ten thousand persons took oaths of allegiance at his hand in a single day. The number of his followers rose day by day and thousands of non-Muslims embraced Islam. Innumerable persons repented of their past sins. Within a short period of five or six years about thirty hundred thousand persons took the *bi'at* on his hands, while, on his way to the *haj* another hundred thousand men took

1. *Sawāneh Ahmadi*.
2. Wiliāyat 'Ali was a respected leader and precursor of the people who claim to follow the Traditions of the Prophet rather than one of the juristic schools. The esteem in which he held the Saiyid is apparent from the above quotation. Another great leader of the sect, Shāh Muhammad Ismā'il, has paid a glowing tribute to his spiritual mentor, Saiyid Ahmad Shahid, in the introduction to his book *Sirāt-i-Mustaqim*.

the oath. Thousands of these were scholars, those who had committed the Qur'ān to their memorary, expert jurists and men distinguished in other fields of life. All this goes to show that God had blessed him with such a popularity that everybody felt his heart attracted to him ." [1]

Wilāyāt 'Alī goes on further to describe the change brought about in the life of those who joined the Saiyid's movement.

"One ought to know the salubrious influence exerted by the company of these pious men. Whosoever joins them with a sincere heart and takes the *bi'at* to the Saiyid, he instantly feels an aversion to the world and develops a liking for the hereafter. This goes on increasing till he is completely cut adrift from polytheistic practices and innovations ; love and regard for God and admiration for the *sharī'ah* increases ; eagerness for the prayer takes root into his heart ; everyone set against God falls into dis-favour no matter whether he is father or son, daughter or mentor ; the awe of God allowes no cordiality to them. Many of them give up their vocations, leave callings disallowed by the *sharī'ah* and desert their homes for the sake of God. These men have persuaded most of the people to offer prayers with the result that the snivelling charlatans are demanding their followers to perform the prayers

1. Wilāyat 'Ali, *Risā'il Tis'a*, Delhi, N. D. p. 56.

lest they should turn away from them."[1]

Karāmat 'Alī of Jaunpur (b. 1209 A. H.) was one of the greatest reformers India has seen. The marvellous success of his missionary endeavour in Bengal, where he created the zeal for faith in millions, bears testimony to his saintliness.[2]   He writes about the Saiyid :

"It is not necessary to describe his winsome qualities for they are known to all in the country. What else can be a greater miracle than the entire population taking to religious observances at his behest ? Aforetime even the women folk of religious-minded people paid no attention to prayer, but now the men and women belonging to every cast and class perform the prayers punctually. people now recit the Qur'an correctly and there is such a zeal for committing the Book of God to one's memory that even women, in the villages and towns, are memorising it. The older mosques are now filled with the worshippers and new ones are being constructed. Thousands among the populace have perfomed the *haj :* polytheistic usages and practices have been given up ; the demand for religious books has increased and even the rare treatises can now be found in every village and habitation. Of a fact, the Saiyid is the spiritual guide of entire Muslim community of the

1.   *Risā'il Tis'a*, p. 66.
2.   The author heard Nawāb Bahādur Yār Jang saying in one of his speeches that Karāmat 'Alī·guided twenty million people to the path of righteousness in Bengal.

day.   One may know it or not, acknowledge or refute it, but the fact is that entry in the fold one who has been made a Renovator by God, is the sign of one's own strength of faith.[1]"

Acknowledgement by Some Orientalists

Notwithsanding the smearing campaign and distortion of facts, mentioned above, by most of the Western writers, some of them have acknowledged the extensiveness of Saiyid's *Jihād* Movement as well as the lasting effect it had on the Muslim society of Indo-Pak sub-continent.   Wilfred Cantwell Smith who has studied the various Islamic revivalist movements of different countries calling the Muslims back to Islam, writes in the *Islam in the Modern History:*

"Even more lasting and more widespread was the persistence of the movement's impetus and ideal. The attempts to oust the infidel could be, and were, suppressed. The attempts to refine and renew Muslim society and to restore its glory must continue, and incidently keep it reminded of its more proper destiny on both scores. The dream of revived Indo-Muslim power remained into the twentieth century, to haunt or incite the community".[2]

1.   Karamat Ali, *Makashafāt-i-Rahmat*
2.   Wilfred Cantwell Smith, *Islam in Modern History*, (Mentor Books 1957), p. 53.

Another Western scholar, P. Hardy, writing about the objectives and mass appeal of the Saiyid's *Jihād* Movement, says:

"Saiyid Ahmad of Bareilly aimed not to restore the Mughals or the Mughal aristocracy, but to create a facsimile of the early Muslim community on the borders of India, in the belief that it would one day inspire Muslims to conquer India for God. His message appealed not to the higher but to the humbler strata of Muslim society in India, to the lower middle classes of pre-Industrial society, to petty landlords, country-town mullahs, to teachers, book-sellers, small shopkeepers, minor officials and skilled artisans."[1]

The Prophet's Deputy and Imam

The time has come, perhaps, when this great reformer and renovator of Islam should be assigned his rightful place in the history of Islam. It would need a deep study and re-evaluation of his reformatory efforts, of his sacrifices made for renewal of the true concept of *jihad* and his influence on the subsequent Muslim thought in a responsible manner as the duty owed to him by the entire world of Islam. It would need to bring into light his greatness—the sublime objectives he had set before himself, his reformatory and missionary planning and his strategy of war, his vaulting ambition, his large-heartedness and his

1. P. Hardy, *The Muslims of British India*, Cambridge, 1972, p. 58

sagacity and wisdom—which has been concealed from the gaze of the Islamic World by the heavy mist of misunderstanding. The World of Islam needs his light to derive inspiration from him.

But, an appreciation of the Saiyid's true worth and significance depends on a correct understanding of the Quranic verse which says :

"Allah verily hath shown grace to the believers by sending unto them a messenger of their own who reciteth unto them His revelations, and causeth them to grow, and teacheth them the Scripture and wisdom ; although before (he came to them) they were in flagrant error."[1]

What this means is that one who undertakes this task should be aware of the transcendental nature of *dīn* : the religion of God ; its extensive range and the depth of its reach ; the inter-relationship between *dīn*, on the one hand, and faith, worship, morals, purification of self and propinquity to God, on the other ; for, they jointly form the bases of law and politics, guidance and government in Islam. He should have also understood Islam in the way it was presented and practised by the holy Prophet, his companions and their successors and should reject the distinctions drawn between inner essence and extrinsic form of religion, between the matter and spirit, between religion and politics, and should reject the sweeping speculations of the Western philosophers about religious truth which are logical, though unconscious,

___

1. Q. III : 164

products of a materialistic and speculative philosophy. Such a man can alone do justice to that shining light who deserves a place among the greatest sons of Islam, its saints and reformers, its leaders and fighters for God.

The character of Saiyid Ahmad Shahīd, his understanding of Islam and his endeavour to present it in its real and original form reflects his deep study of the Qur'ān and loving devotion to the holy Prophet. These had got imprinted on his spirit and had become his inward instinct. Truly speaking, he had been guided and groomed by God for taking the place of a reformer and renovator needed by the time. The Age in which he was born needed a guide who was truthful and sincere, selfless and pure of heart ; who hated fame and riches, the worldly objects and desires ; who had given himself up completely in the hands of God ; who depended on prayer and supplication and beseechment to his Lord ; since, only a man with these dispositions and qualities could revive the spirit of faith in the despondent and depressed people of his time. He was not, and should never be equated with the national, racial and political leaders or conquerors and builders of empires or else the founders of political parties.

Those who are familiar with the prophetic mood and disposition—a characteristic visible *par excellance* in the last of the prophets, Muhammad, but common to all of them—and understands the likes and dislikes, character and behaviour, orisons and prayers, policies and politics of the apostles of God can alone realise their heartache, the restlessness of their spirit and the reason for their sleepless nights. He can comprehend why they wandered like a man mad after his mission, why they never cared for the world, what it was that gave effectiveness to their speech, why their eyes were so often brimmed with tears and why it was that a sentence or two coming from their lips turned the evil-doers into saints and enemies into friends.

One who understands this prophetic mood and disposition would automatically understand them and their character. It is the only key that can open up the secret of their personalities which is still a closed book for those scholars and writers who cannot free themselves from the modern materialistic way of thought, its standards and values

"And, verily. Allah guideth whom He will unto the straight path."[1]

The Saiyid, leadership provides a living, real and unhampered guidance which is always needed and looked for by wise and foresighted men in the *millat*. For this is the only elixir needed for the ills of the Muslims in every country and Age. It was correctly understood by the Poet of the East, who poetized this fact in these words.

The reality of *Imāmat* thou asketh me,
May God let thee perceive the secrets I know.
He is, verily, the *Imām* of his time,
Who makes thee shun the existent and the present.

1. Q. II : 213.

Showing the face of beloved in the mirror of death,
Makes thy life still more difficult to endure.

By letting thee look into thy abasement, makes thy
blood boil,

Turns thee into a sword by making thee indifferent
to the world.

Calamity for the *millat* is the leadership of one,
Who makes the Muslims an adorer of the kings.

9 798824 651010